Haiku

The Travelers of Eternity

Haiku

The Travelers of Eternity

Haiku by Charles Ghigna

Sumi-e (Ink Paintings) by Armor Keller

RIVER CITY PUBLISHING
Montgomery, Alabama

Haiku copyright © 2001 by Charles Ghigna
Sumi-e copyright © 2001 by Armor Keller

All rights reserved under International and Pan-American Copyright
Conventions. Published in the United States by River City Publishing LLC, P.O.
Box 551, Montgomery, AL 36101.

Library of Congress Cataloging-in-Publication Data:

Ghigna, Charles.
  Haiku : the travelers of eternity / haiku by Charles Ghigna ; sumi-e (ink
paintings) by Armor Keller.
      p. cm.
   ISBN 0-913515-15-9 (alk. paper)
   1. Haiku, American. 2. Nature--Poetry. 3. Months--Poetry. I.
Keller, Armor. II. Title.
   PS3557.H5 H35 2001
   811'.54--dc21
   2001000353

                    Designed by Lissa Monroe.
                      Printed in Korea.

River City Publishing publishes works by distinguished Southern authors
and artists. Our imprints include River City, Starrhill, Sycamore, and
Black Belt.

The Haiku

The Japanese haiku, one of the oldest forms of poetic expression, teaches us much about the art and craft of poem-making. The entire poem consists of only seventeen syllables in three short lines of five-seven-five syllables, yet the haiku contains all the basic elements of poetry.

The haiku is understated and concise. It is lyrical and dramatic, poignant and precise, personal and universal. Sometimes it is witty. But always it is ethereal and timeless, as meaningful today as it was hundreds of years ago when Basho, Buson, Issa, and the other masters of haiku first began exploring its potential as an art form.

The haiku of this collection employ the traditional use of seasonal imagery to portray the cyclical aspect of nature and time.

—Charles Ghigna

The Art of Sumi-e

Sumi-e is the Japanese word for the art of black-ink paint-ing. It is a medium that embodies the aesthetic for things just hinted at or suggested. Because sumi-e is created with very few brush strokes, it is sometimes referred to as the "haiku of painting."

The term *sumi-e* refers to both the technique and the medium. The painting is done with sumi, an ink that is ground from a solid ink stick immediately before paint-ing. This is done by rubbing the stick against a stone (called a *suzuri*) in water. The longer the ink is ground, the darker the shade of the color.

Sumi-e can be applied to silk and to a variety of papers. A special type of brush is required. It must have enough soft hairs to hold the ink, and enough stiff hairs to spring back to a point at the end of every stroke. The strokes must be clear, balanced, and confident.

On the silk or paper, the sumi looks similar to watercolor, but unlike watercolor it is permanent. Because this does not allow for reworking or correcting mistakes, imperfect paintings are destroyed.

—Armor Keller

The months and days are the travelers of eternity.

—Basho

Spring

April

Ivory butterflies
perch on black branches,
the dogwood blossoms.

May

The cherry blossom
wakes, stretches, opens herself
to the morning sun.

June

The cricket calls to
the meadow, each evening he
hears his echo sing.

Summer

July

Beyond fields of rice
shadows sway to moonlight's breeze,
lithe bamboo dancers.

August

Listen, the forest
waits for summer's final song,
the whippoorwill sings.

September

Shadows bow to the
setting sun, pray to the sky
for blessings of light.

Fall

October

Artist autumn comes,
paints her blush across each tree,
drops palette, and leaves.

November

Geese fly south pulling
over the mountaintops a
stone curtain of sky.

December

The last lullaby,
an owl cries out through the pines,
the north wind answers.

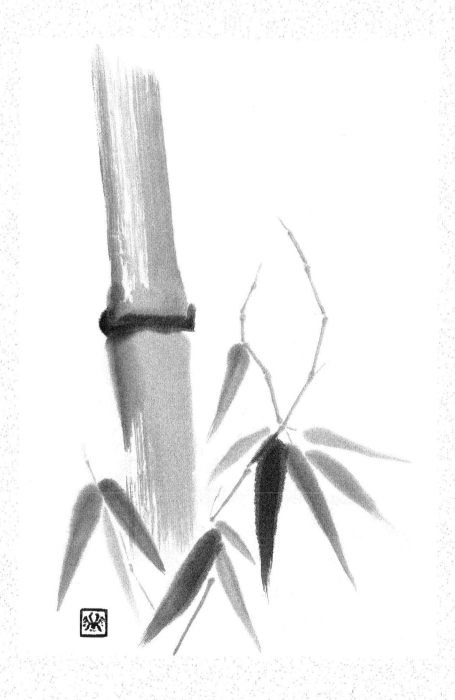

Winter

January

A sleeping doe stirs
beneath her blanket of dawn,
a new year rising.

February

The sea lion roars
across the far horizon,
storm clouds stalk the shore.

March

A field full of pale
parachutes, dandelions
adrift in the wind.